PIZARRO
CONQUEROR OF PERU

PIZARRO
CONQUEROR OF PERU

by William Jay Jacobs

Franklin Watts
New York / Chicago / London / Toronto / Sydney
A First Book

Cover illustration by Amy Wasserman
Cover photograph copyright © Archive Photos, NYC
Cover map copyright © North Wind Picture Archives, Alfred, Me.
Map on page 25 by Gary S. Tong

Photographs copyright ©: Photo Researchers, Inc./ARCHIV: p. 2;
Robert Frerck/Odyssey/ Chicago: pp. 10, 13, 18, 44, 46; Stock Montage/Historical
Pictures Service: pp. 15, 53; North Wind Picture Archives: pp. 20, 28, 30, 32, 35, 38,
52, 55; New York Public Library, Picture Collection: pp. 23, 39, 47, 50; Ancient Art &
Architecture Collection: p. 42.

Library of Congress Cataloging-in-Publication Data

Jacobs, William Jay.
Pizarro, conqueror of Peru / by William Jay Jacobs.
p. cm. — (A First book)
Includes bibliographical references and index.
ISBN 0-531-20107-4
1. Pizarro, Francisco, ca. 1475–1541 — Juvenile literature.
2. Peru — History — Conquest, 1522–1548 — Juvenile literature.
3. Conquerors — Peru — Biography — Juvenile literature. 4. Conquerors—Spain —
Biography—Juvenile literature. 5. Explorers — Peru—Biography — Juvenile literature. 6. Explorers—Spain—Biography—Juvenile literature. [1. Pizarro, Francisco, ca.
1475–1541. 2. Explorers. 3. Peru—Discovery and exploration.] I. Title. II. Series.
F3442.P776J33 1994
985'.02'092—dc20   93-31158
[B]   CIP AC

Copyright © 1994 by William Jay Jacobs
All rights reserved
Printed in the United States of America
6 5 4 3 2 1

CONTENTS

He stared out at the Pacific — and all his men
Looked at each other with a wild surmise —
Silent, upon a peak in Darien.
                              — JOHN KEATS

Gold! Gold! Gold! Gold!
Bright and yellow, hard and cold.
                              — THOMAS HOOD

FOREWORD
TO A
REMARKABLE
STORY

Francisco Pizarro was born to poverty, the child of parents who never married. To the end of his life, he learned neither how to read nor how to write. Yet, once, as a soldier in the conquering Spanish army on the isthmus of Panama, he heard a native tell a story that would come to change the course of human history. The Indian said that in a country across "the narrow place" [close to today's Panama Canal] and "along the great South Sea" lay a land where people "drink from golden cups and eat on golden dishes."

Pizarro was deeply moved to hear the Indian's tale. He dreamed that he would one day sail to the south and visit that great golden kingdom, known as "Biru" (or "Piru"). Then, after finding it, he would conquer and rule it.

In 1532, with fewer than two hundred soldiers at his command, Pizarro set out to conquer the rich and glorious empire of the ancient Incas. To the deeply religious Christians who later became members of Pizarro's

9

The promise of riches beyond belief,
such as this ceremonial golden knife,
drew the Spanish to South America.

army, their task had the blessing of God. True, they sought glory, along with gold, but to those ferocious Spanish conquistadores (or conquerors), victory over the Incas, no matter how brutal or how violent, had a holy purpose. Thus, it was justified.

Despite the period of blood and greed that followed Pizarro's dramatic triumph over the Inca leader, Atahualpa, the Spanish success was destined to become one of history's most important events. It would shape future events in much of the continent now known to us as South America.

CHAPTER ONE
A
DREAM
OF
CONQUEST

Francisco Pizarro was born in Trujillo, Spain, in the province of Estremadura. Although the actual date is uncertain, most historians believe that he was born about 1471. At the time, his parents were not married, and they made little effort to record the event exactly. His father, Gonzalo Pizarro, was a colonel in the Spanish infantry. His mother, it is said, was a prostitute.

According to stories of the day, after Pizarro's birth his mother abandoned him at the entrance to a church. In fact, he probably was raised by his grandparents along with his half brothers. In early childhood, like many children of the day, he spent his time on a farm caring for the pigs. As a teenager, he enlisted in the army. Through his twenties and early thirties he served faithfully, but with little success and little advancement in rank. Perhaps because of that, he decided to sign into service on a ship bound for the New World, leaving his Spanish homeland behind him without regret.

In 1502, Pizarro served on the island of Hispaniola

*This statue of Pizarro stands in
his hometown, Trujillo, Spain.*

(today's Haiti and Dominican Republic). Later, he took part in a campaign in Colombia. Most exciting of all to him, Pizarro shared in the successful struggle of Hernando Cortés to overthrow Montezuma's Aztec empire in Mexico. Then he helped to organize the settlement at Darien, on the eastern coast of Panama. From there he accompanied the heroic explorer, Balboa, on a painful crossing of the mountains, emerging at last to behold the spectacular South Sea, known today as the Pacific Ocean.

Because of his loyal service and his good judgment, Pizarro began to advance swiftly in rank. Yet, acting under orders from Spain, Pizarro did not hesitate to help arrest his own gallant commander and friend, Balboa. He then stood by and watched as an executioner put an end to the life of the great Spanish discoverer.

In 1522, already past the age of fifty, Pizarro became mayor of the town of Panama. By then he was modestly wealthy. Yet, increasingly, he thought of himself as a "conquistador without a conquest." Still eager for wealth as well as glory, he began to plan a voyage to the south, to lands where it was rumored there was much gold. To help him achieve his dream he turned to two companions: a fellow warrior, Diego de Almagro, and a wealthy priest, Hernando de Luque.

The infant Almagro had been abandoned at the entrance to a church by his natural parents. Like Pizarro, he had never learned to read and write. Yet he

*Balboa discovered the Pacific Ocean
in September 1513.*

eventually became known as a gallant soldier, as well as a man of charm and ambition.

Father Luque, much younger than either Pizarro or Almagro, had long served as a schoolmaster in Darien. He was highly respected in the Spanish New World community. Even more important to the other two adventurers, he was a man of considerable wealth. And buying arms, ammunition, food, and ships required much money.

Together, the three men agreed to explore the uncharted lands to the south, to take possession of them, and then to divide equally the vast fortune they were certain would be theirs. Each of the three had a task: Luque was to arrange for financing their efforts; Almagro was to recruit soldiers and organize the expedition; and Pizarro was to be the chief soldier, leading the Spanish forces into action.

In November 1524, Pizarro set sail from Panama with a force of only 140 soldiers and sailors aboard two ships. Almagro, it was agreed, would follow afterward with additional forces. Never did the three planners dream that eight full years would pass before the Inca capital would finally fall into their hands.

CHAPTER TWO
EAST MEETS WEST:
THE DISCOVERY
OF THE
INCA CIVILIZATION

Pizarro's first voyage to the south, begun in 1524, proved largely to be a failure. Storms and swirling seas slowed the progress of his ships. After the Spaniards landed, the natives they met fled from them in fear. Soon all of the explorers' food was gone. They ate bitter fruits from the trees. Finally, they were reduced to boiling the leather of their sword belts and trying to use them for food.

Deciding to go inland from the seacoast, the Spaniards fell into an Indian ambush. Five Spanish soldiers died in the attack, and Pizarro, despite his armor, was wounded in seven places. Eventually the Spaniards managed to drive back their attackers. Meanwhile, Almagro, Pizarro's partner, had followed him southward in another vessel but could not find him. Native forces also attacked Almagro. In one battle, they wounded the Spanish leader with a javelin. As a result, he lost sight in one eye.

Still, neither Pizarro nor Almagro was discouraged. By the time they finally met, both had managed to col-

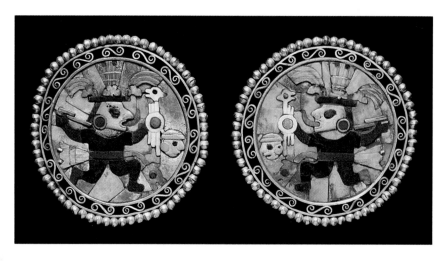

*Beautiful golden ear ornaments depicting victorious warriors
and their victims' heads were some of the many treasures
of the people living in Peru at the time Pizarro arrived.*

lect modest supplies of gold from their conquests. Both
had also been told that much greater wealth lay farther
to the south in the hands of a great empire.

Returning to Panama, the two warriors immediately began to plan another voyage along the southern
coast. They signed a formal contract with Father
Luque, promising to share with him the profits of the
coming expedition. Clearly, gold was their objective.
But Father Luque blessed their mission, no matter
what it cost in lives, in the name of the triumph of
Christianity and the conversion of the surviving natives
to that religion. In exchange for advancing 20,000

pesos to his partners, Luque would receive one-third of the expected treasure.

In 1526, Pizarro and Almagro took to the sea once again. This time their fleet included two large ships and eight smaller ones. After cruising along the coastline, they stopped at a small village where they captured several natives along with many gold ornaments. Sailing farther south, they stumbled upon villages filled with even more gold and precious jewels. Some of the Indians wore pearl necklaces. They poured gold powder over their fingers and even wore golden studs in their cheeks.

Few of the natives were friendly to the advancing Spaniards. Therefore, seeing the need for still more Spanish soldiers, Almagro returned to Panama. He carried with him appealing golden trinkets intended to tempt young warriors to join the mission. When he arrived, however, Almagro discovered to his surprise that a new Spanish governor had taken over. Instead of supporting the expedition, the governor soon sent a message to the troops. They should all, he urged, return at once to Panama. If Pizarro wished to continue on his insane expedition southward he was allowed to do so, but without official support!

Many of the Spanish soldiers admired Pizarro greatly. They saw that he always plunged into combat first, at the head of his forces. They had watched him sleep on the bare ground, along with all the other men.

Pizzaro draws his famous "line in the sand"
and urges his soldiers to follow him to Peru.

But they also knew that he spoke little, never laughed, and strictly enforced obedience to his commands. The soldiers respected him, yet at the same time feared him.

After hearing the governor's message, Pizarro waited. There was silence. Then, suddenly, Pizarro drew a dagger from his belt and rushed like a tiger to the front of his forces. With his knife, he firmly drew a line in the sand extending from east to west. Then, pointing to the south, he shouted: "Comrades, to that side, to the south, are toil, hunger, nakedness, the drenching storm, desertion, and death; on this side, ease and pleasure. There lies Peru and its riches, here Panama and its

20

poverty. Choose, Castilians.... For my own part, I go to the south!" With that, Pizarro leaped across the line he had drawn, openly defying the governor.

At first there was silence among his men. Then one of them, the expedition's navigator, Bartolomé Ruiz, joined Pizarro. Another man followed. Then another, until at last thirteen soldiers stood beside their commander. Almost every member of the daring little cluster was destined to win great fame, as well as a fortune in gold.

That moment proved to be a turning point in Pizarro's life. Had he simply accepted the view of the governor, it is unlikely that his name would be remembered today as among history's most triumphant military figures and as one who devastated an existing culture.

Ruiz, the navigator, agreed to pilot Pizarro's ship back to Panama, delivering the soldiers who had chosen to obey the governor. Seven months later he returned, accompanied by a new force of conquistadores.

Sailing to the south, the Spaniards finally landed at the city of Tumbes, beyond the equator. To the natives there, the bearded, light-skinned Spaniards, with their great ship and shiny metal weapons, seemed almost godlike.

Using all the charm at his command, Pizarro provided the Tumbes chief with an iron hatchet, something the Indians had never seen before. They, in turn, served the Spaniards food on gold and silver platters and then brought them to temples coated with gold and silver decorations.

Pizarro, controlling the greed of his soldiers, simply gave his thanks to the natives for their hospitality. At first he refused the gifts of gold that both he and his men so much desired. Yet when at last he departed from Tumbes it was with several vases filled to their rims with gold and silver. He brought with him, too, three tribesmen, by then referred to by the Spaniards as "Peruvians." One of the men, named "Felipillo" by the Spanish soldiers, was destined to play an important role in the coming adventures of Pizarro.

Returning at once to Panama, Pizarro was shocked when the Spanish governor refused to take his adventure seriously, even dismissing the treasures he delivered as a "cheap display of gold and silver toys...." To Pizarro's companions, Luque and Almagro, it soon became clear that there was only one path to the achievement of their dream. They must return to Spain, where they could speak in person with Charles V, who was both king of Spain and Holy Roman Emperor.

But who would make the trip? Luque could not be spared from his critical religious duties in Panama. Almagro was far too plain and blunt a speaker to deal with royalty and, besides, had lost an eye in combat. Pizarro, it is true, could neither read nor write, but he was a man of commanding athletic appearance who spoke confidently and convincingly. Although Luque did

*King of Spain and Holy Roman
Emperor Charles V depicted
in a painting by Titian*

not altogether trust his ambitions, it soon was decided that he would be the trio's representative in Spain.

So it was in the spring of 1528 that Francisco Pizarro said farewell to his comrades and departed for the court of King Charles.

CHAPTER THREE
ON THE BRINK:
TRIUMPH
OR
DEATH

When Pizarro first left Spain, more than a quarter of a century earlier, he had been young, unknown, and poor. In the spring of 1528, that same child, now a man, knelt at Toledo before the throne of the world's most powerful ruler, Charles V.

While Pizarro spoke slowly and carefully about his adventures in the Americas, King Charles held in his hand a packet of jewels from Peru. He caressed the fleece of a Peruvian llama and studied roughly drawn maps of the Pacific coastline. Pizarro described, too, the vast storehouses of gold that could soon belong to Spain.

But the clever conquistador also pointed out to his ruler how, along with immense new lands for Spain, entire nations of people could be won over to a belief in Jesus Christ. Pizarro then told in simple words how he and only thirteen other soldiers somehow had managed to survive on their own in the distant land of Peru. At that point, the king was reduced to tears.

Greatly impressed, Charles agreed in principle to support Pizarro's plan. Several months later, while

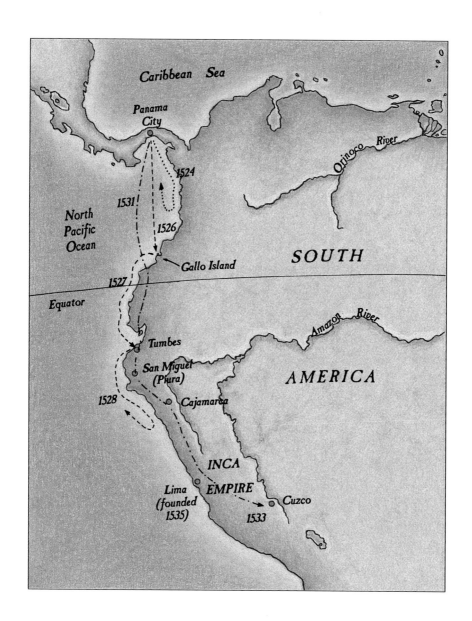

Caribbean Sea

Panama City

1524

1531

North Pacific Ocean

1526

Gallo Island

1527

Equator

Orinoco River

SOUTH

Amazon River

Tumbes

San Miguel (Piura)

1528

Cajamarca

AMERICA

INCA

EMPIRE

Lima (founded 1535)

1533

Cuzco

Pizarro's journey through Peru

25

Charles was away, the queen signed a formal agreement granting Pizarro the right to conquer Peru. He was granted the title of governor of the settlements there, as well as responsibility for maintaining law and order in the new Spanish colonies. In return for his great and loyal services to the nation, he was to receive a highly generous salary of 725,000 maravedís a year.

Pizarro's comrades, Almagro, Luque, and Ruiz were also given responsibilities and titles of command, but their rewards were far less than those of Pizarro, both in money and in power. Almagro was given the least: only 100,000 maravedís and command of a fortress at Tumbes.

Proud of successful dealings with the nation's rulers, Pizarro returned to Trujillo, his birthplace in Spain. There, he had once been part of the lowest class. Now the townspeople greeted him warmly and applauded him. He proudly displayed to his childhood friends the medals given to him by the king. He also recruited men to serve with him in his campaign to conquer Peru.

Four of his half brothers agreed to join the expedition. Two of them, young Gonzalo and Juan Pizarro, were destined to become daring, popular commanders. Another half brother, Martín, would become Pizarro's own loyal and devoted assistant, one day giving his own life to protect the great Spanish explorer from assassination.

His fourth half brother, Hernando Pizarro, would become Francisco's most trusted friend and closest adviser. Older than the others and far better educated, he was greedy both for money and for power. In later years, to gain his personal ends he would do any deed — not only to the natives, whom he treated with bloodthirsty hatred, but to his own Spanish comrades.

A fifth relative, fifteen-year-old Pedro Pizarro, joined the group as a page. It was Pedro who one day would write a history of the incredible events that soon were to take place.

In January 1530, with three ships under his command, Pizarro departed from Spain. When finally he arrived in Panama, Luque and Almagro awaited him on the dock. Almagro in particular was furious to learn how small a share of the coming conquest he was to receive. He bitterly condemned Pizarro for breaking his word. Only after Luque convinced Pizarro to pledge an equal division of the profits among the three (following a deduction of the emperor's usual one-fifth share) did Almagro once again begin to smile.

One year later Pizarro was finally prepared to set sail to the south, bound for Peru. Before his three ships left the harbor, the bishop of Panama blessed the fleet and the Spanish soldiers, praying for their safety. Almagro, who was to remain behind to recruit more troops, took holy communion alongside Pizarro. Then, as the three vessels departed, the crews on board

Sturdy Spanish galleons
transported the conquistadores
to the New World.

solemnly joined together in singing a religious hymn.
The struggle for the conquest of Peru had begun.

After two weeks at sea, slowed by unfavorable
winds, the conquistadores decided to proceed by land.
In the province of Coaque, they were received by
friendly natives. The Spaniards, however, looted the villages they came upon. Pizarro distributed to his men

their share of the booty while setting aside the one-fifth portion reserved for the emperor. Much of the rest — gold and silver and precious gems — he sent back to Panama and to neighboring Nicaragua, hoping to attract more soldiers to his force.

Before long, a force of thirty men joined him, led by the courageous Sebastián de Belalcázar. Already the Spaniards had suffered from windstorms, swirling sands, and attacks by native tribes. Many soldiers tried to treat serious cactus sores by lancing them with knives to ease the pain. For some, the result was infection and death.

Then, just as the rainy season began, the valiant Spanish leader, Hernando De Soto, arrived from Nicaragua with two more ships and one hundred men. Pizarro was delighted. Not only was De Soto from Pizarro's own Spanish province, Estremadura, he was also a daring swordsman and extraordinary horseman, always admired by his troops.

While waiting for the end of the rainy season, Pizarro learned from local Indians of the bloody struggle for power that had just taken place in Peru. One of two brothers, Huáscar, had inherited the throne following the death of his father, the eleventh "Lord Inca" in Peru. But the jealous Huáscar feared the ambition of his half brother, a talented soldier named Atahualpa. The result had been a terrible conflict that took the lives of thousands of men on the battlefields of Peru.

Hernando De Soto

Shortly before Pizarro's arrival Atahualpa's armies had triumphed and he had become the Inca king, with Huáscar as his prisoner. Immediately, he ordered his officers in the capital city of Cuzco to kill Huáscar's family. Before the very eyes of the former ruler, his own brothers, sisters, wives, and children were murdered. Then their bodies were hung on stakes in the city's central square for all to see. After that, the Incas known to be followers of Huáscar were dragged from their homes and, in public view, cruelly tortured to death.

Having heard about those events, Pizarro rapidly made his way southward. In some cities such as Tumbes, he discovered that much of the gold, silver, and precious jewels had been removed during the war between the two brothers. Still, Pizarro continued on. At one point he called his army together. Then he announced that, before the coming conflict, all those who wished to leave were free to go. Nine men chose to return to Panama. To the 168 who remained, it was perfectly clear that there could be no retreat. What lay ahead was either victory or death.

Learning that Atahualpa's force was encamped at the city of Cajamarca, Pizarro decided to meet him there at once. The daring path that the Spanish conquistador then chose lay across the mighty Andes, one of the world's highest mountain ranges. Some of his officers urged a longer, easier route, but Pizarro refused.

Upward the Spanish forces climbed, along narrow pathways to cold and snowy heights. All around them loomed icy glaciers. Sometimes the horses had to be forced across ledges extending over ravines hundreds of feet below. Many of the soldiers feared an Inca ambush, but no one dared to question the commands of Pizarro.

At last, the Spaniards reached the summit, where only flights of condors soared. Then they began their

*Pizarro and his troop's daring journey through
the narrow perilous passes high in the Andes
Mountains on his way to meet Atahualpa*

32

descent to the valley of Cajamarca below. Soon they could see a flowing river and cultivated farmlands. They could also see the houses nestling together in a city. Seven days after beginning their historic climb, the Spanish force finally neared its goal. Then, to their amazement, they saw in the mountains on the other side of the valley a vast array of tents, certainly numbering in the thousands. It was the army of Atahualpa!

First Pizarro was greeted by a messenger from the Inca monarch, bearing gifts and asking when the Spaniards would arrive in Cajamarca. A second messenger arrived later, urging the strangers to proceed no further. But for Pizarro, there was no turning back. Despite the enormous force of Inca warriors gathered before him, he ordered his small band of soldiers into battle formation.

With armored horsemen in the lead, their colorful flags fluttering in the breeze, the Spanish conquistadores descended toward the city spread out below them.

The date was November 15, 1532. From that day onward the history of Spain as well as of South America never again would be the same.

CHAPTER FOUR

TWO CIVILIZATIONS FACE-TO-FACE

Echoes filled the air as the hooves of the Spanish cavalry clattered along the streets of Cajamarca. Otherwise there was silence. All the Inca inhabitants of Cajamarca had withdrawn from the city.

Pizarro did not hesitate. Quickly he dispatched his brother, Hernando, along with Hernando De Soto, to meet with Atahualpa in the camp of the Incas, some 3 miles (4.8 km) from the city. Following behind the two Spanish leaders rode twenty white-skinned warriors on horseback, clad in shining, clanking armor, trumpets blasting into the air to announce their passage.

When they arrived at the emperor's camp, Atahualpa at first remained completely silent as the bold conquistadores spoke to him. But De Soto noticed how often the Inca ruler glanced with interest at his fiery war-horse. Leaping into the saddle, the daring Spaniard dashed across the plain, skillfully wheeling his horse about. Then he charged directly toward Atahualpa, stopping just before the still unsmiling

34

Spaniards at Cajamarca, the camp
of the Incan leader Atahualpa

ruler's body. Several of Atahualpa's guards drew back in fear as the horse came near. And for that the Inca leader had them executed the very same night.

Nor were the Spaniards entirely hopeful as they returned to Cajamarca, making their way before the eyes of thousands of silently gazing natives. Pizarro, however, expressed pleasure. At last, he said, they had come face-to-face with Atahualpa. Now, they must capture him, just as Cortés had captured the Aztec leader, Montezuma, in Mexico.

Atahualpa had promised De Soto to visit the Spaniards at Cajamarca the next day, and Pizarro prepared carefully for the Inca leader's coming. At two entrances leading to the city's central square he stationed horsemen, one group commanded by De Soto, the other by Hernando Pizarro. At a third entrance he stationed foot soldiers.

The night before, the Spaniards had joined together by torchlight to celebrate a Roman Catholic Mass. They prayed that, as conquistadores, they would serve as soldiers of God. At lunchtime on November 16, the Spaniards ate a formal meal, ending with final prayers for victory. Then they took their battle stations.

Just before sunset Atahualpa arrived. At first the Inca ruler sent a messenger, saying that he would enter the city in the morning. But Pizarro feared that his own troops would become restless and lose confidence. He sent a message — completely untrue — that he had prepared a special banquet for Atahualpa. It would be unfortunate if the Inca leader did not join him.

Nightfall had yet to come when Atahualpa agreed to Pizarro's request. He ordered his group, composed of five or six thousand lightly armed men, to enter the town square. Three thousand Incas clothed in red prepared the way for their monarch and his forces, chanting as they swept the streets with palm leaves. They, in turn, were followed by warriors dressed in blue — men from the noblest Inca families. Finally, Atahualpa himself appeared, carried on a shining golden throne. On his head he wore a crown, with black and white plumes extending upward from it. And around his neck hung a band of sparkling emeralds. Yet not a single Spaniard stood in the courtyard to greet him.

When Atahualpa asked aloud where the strangers were, there emerged a single Spaniard, Friar Vicente de Valverde, holding a Christian cross in his hand. At his side walked the young native, Felipillo, or "Little Philip," who by then had come to know Spanish well. Valverde spoke at length about the Christian religion and how Emperor Charles V had appointed Pizarro to conquer the Incas and bring that religion to them. The native people, said Valverde, had no choice but to surrender.

Atahualpa answered softly that the band of strangers was not right in trying to force their beliefs on his people. Nor had they been kind to the Incas they had met so far, robbing them of gold and silver. Then,

ATHABALIBA
ultimus Rex Peruanorum

*The young Incan leader, Atahualpa,
the last Inca king of Peru*

Atahualpa being captured by the Spaniards. The priest explained to him that King Charles V had sent Pizarro to conquer the Incas and to convert them to Christianity.

turning the pages of the Bible that Valverde advanced to him, he angrily threw it to the ground. Valverde picked up the book and hurried inside.

Having watched the entire scene, Pizarro knew it was the moment he had waited for. As planned with his men, he waved a white scarf in the air. From a nearby fortress, a single shot responded to his signal. Instantly, Spanish gunners began to fire their powerful cannons. Mounted cavalry charged boldly into the city square. Lancers cut into the crowded mass of Peruvians.

In the first few minutes, hundreds of Incas died. Cannons continued to take a frightful toll as Spanish riders on horseback eagerly followed Inca warriors trying desperately to escape from the horrible bloodletting. Atahualpa's personal defenders gathered around his throne, only to be slashed to death by the Spaniards. Finally, Pizarro himself dragged the Inca leader to safety, suffering a slash-wound as he did so. It was, in fact, the only injury among all the Spanish soldiers. At least two thousand Incas lost their lives, possibly even more.

Afterward, the conquistadores searched the bodies strewn about the square, joyfully gathering gold and silver objects. Hundreds of women were taken captive. For some of the Spaniards, after pursuing the dream of conquest for eight years, it was their moment of glory.

In the hills nearby, at entrances to the valley where the city of Cajamarca nestled, thousands of Inca warriors, who had waited to be called, now fled into the night. They left behind them a scene of silence and death. Meanwhile, a triumphant Pizarro stood face-to-face with his captive, Atahualpa.

CHAPTER FIVE

FALL
OF THE
INCA EMPIRE

On the very night of his brilliant success against the Incas, Pizarro arranged for Atahualpa to dine with him. Outside the banquet hall the bodies of Inca warriors still filled the city's central square. At the dining table the smiling Pizarro tried to bring calm to his captive, urging him to have faith in the Spaniards and their gracious God. In response, Atahualpa remained silent.

The next morning Spanish soldiers and their Inca prisoners began to clear the city of corpses. Before long, the conquistadores were surprised to uncover great stockpiles of gold and silver platters for the royal dining tables, as well as huge supplies of emeralds. Now they grew certain that triumph would bring them not only glory, but fantastic wealth.

Hoping that Atahualpa would help him discover still more precious metals, Pizarro placed the monarch in a comfortable residence, allowing him to wear fine clothing and to be served on gold and silver plates by his many wives. He could even speak in private to royal

The Incas offered the Spaniards
rooms filled with gold and silver in
exchange for Atahualpa's freedom.

visitors. Soon the Inca leader learned to play such games as dice and chess. He also came to enjoy the company of his conqueror's brother, Hernando Pizarro, along with that of Hernando De Soto.

What Atahualpa feared most was that his brother, Huáscar, whom he had defeated in battle and imprisoned, might somehow win freedom for himself and once again become the nation's ruler. To prevent that, Atahualpa believed he first had to gain his own freedom. He soon came to understand that Pizarro's passion for gold would be the best way to reach out to his captor. Meanwhile, the Spanish commander had become determined to impress Emperor Charles V with the greatest stockpile of treasure ever before collected, even greater than that returned by Cortes from his conquest of Mexico.

To serve his conqueror's purpose, as well as his own, Atahualpa proposed a deal to Pizarro. In return for his freedom, he promised to fill a room as large as that in which he was imprisoned, nearly 24 feet (7.2 m) long and 18 feet (5.4 m) wide, with *gold*! The Inca monarch raised his arm to a point on the wall as high as he could reach — the gold would be piled that high! Another room, he said, would be filled twice over with silver. Startled at first, Pizarro arranged to have a formal letter of agreement prepared, promising his captive freedom when all of the precious metals were delivered. Never in history, he understood, had there been such a prize.

Soon the precious metals began to arrive: golden plates, silver cups, beautifully shaped ornaments. Daily the treasure mounted. Yet, to Pizarro, the collection of the ransom seemed to be moving too slowly. He feared that massive Inca armies secretly might be gathering to free their ruler. When Atahualpa denied the charge, Pizarro sent soldiers to discover the truth. Some went

Throughout history, gold has brought beauty, as well as tragedy, to human existence. This vase demonstrates the craftsmanship of South American people before the arrival of Europeans.

as far as the Inca capital city, Cuzco, looting it of gold, before returning to say that no revolt was being organized. Atahualpa had, indeed, kept his word.

The Inca monarch now grew fearful. Visitors told him that his brother, Huáscar, still a prisoner in Cuzco, had promised the Spaniards an even greater amount of gold if only Pizarro would free him and restore him to the throne. To Atahualpa, no other news could have seemed so dangerous. A few days later, however, word arrived that Huáscar had been smothered to death in his prison cell, at Atahualpa's command.

Atahualpa's life still remained at risk. The turning point had been the arrival in Cajamarca of Pizarro's partner, Almagro, with a force of 150 men and 84 horses. Almagro immediately demanded his share — one third — of all the profits gained so far. Meanwhile, Almagro and Pizarro's brother, Hernando, continued to hate each other, as they always had before. Pizarro decided that he must act quickly. If he divided the Inca treasure, Almagro would be pleased. He could then send Hernando home to Spain with the share reserved for Charles V. This would separate the quarreling Almagro and Hernando.

But there was another advantage to such a move. Hernando and the Inca leader, Atahualpa, had become close friends. Thus, after Hernando had left for Spain it would be possible to do the terrible deed that now seemed necessary. He would deal in a final way with Atahualpa, who had been promised his freedom once the collection of the treasure was complete. To free so popular a leader, thought Pizarro, could prove too dangerous for the tiny Spanish force.

In August 1533, Pizarro divided the fantastic treasure. By that time, the third conquistador partner, Luque the priest, had died. In a special religious ceremony, the Spaniards gave thanks to God and proceeded

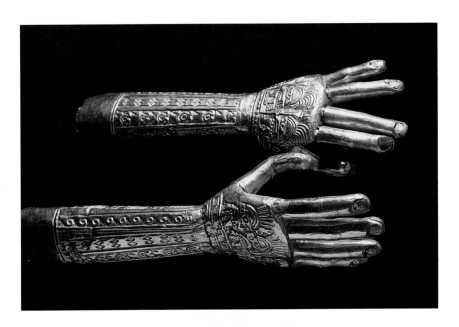

*These pre-Columbian gold arms
were used in funeral ceremonies.*

to distribute a fortune in precious metals. Pizarro himself received the golden throne of Atahualpa. His men received great amounts of gold and silver. Almagro's soldiers accepted less, expecting to receive a larger share after capturing the Inca capital city, Cuzco.

Shortly afterward, Hernando Pizarro left for Spain with the emperor's share of the prize. De Soto, another close friend of Atahualpa, was sent away with a small force, supposedly to see whether reports of Inca troop movements toward Cajamarca were really true. Then, with all of the Inca leader's defenders gone, Pizarro,

46

*Atahualpa was burned to death after
he refused to convert to Christianity.*

instead of freeing Atahualpa as he had promised to do,
placed him on trial.

On August 29, 1533, with De Soto still gone,
Pizarro and Almagro served as trial judges. The mighty
Inca chief was swiftly found guilty of false charges and

47

sentenced to die. That very night, he was to be burned at the stake. As the fires were about to be lighted, Father Valverde offered an easier death to Atahualpa if, at last, he agreed to become a Christian. Instead of burning, he was to be choked to death with a noose. The Inca leader readily agreed. He was then given the Christian name "Juan de Atahualpa" (after John the Baptist). Seeing that no plea could possibly save his life, he faced death with courage and with poise.

As the rope was fastened around his neck Atahualpa stared calmly at Pizarro. Then, while the Spaniards recited prayers for the salvation of his soul, the rope was tightened. Very soon the Inca chieftain died.

Two days later, De Soto returned from his mission. Learning what had happened to Atahualpa, he responded angrily. But it was too late. Atahualpa had passed into history. So, too, had the Inca empire.

Only nine months after descending from the mountains into Cajamarca, Francisco Pizarro, the former swineherd who still could neither read nor write, had strangled the god-king to death and seized a fortune in gold and silver. There, along the coast of South America, in a land almost as large as Western Europe, some 12 million Incas were now in a hopeless situation. They were at the absolute mercy of the cruel Spanish conqueror, Pizarro, along with his small force — fewer than five hundred men — all with pale faces and wearing dazzling suits of armor.

CHAPTER SIX
DISUNITY AND DEATH
FOR THE
SPANISH CONQUERORS

The Incas continued to fight, even after the death of Atahualpa. It became impossible for a Spaniard to travel from city to city without risking his life. Meanwhile, the golden Inca treasures were buried with such secrecy that, to this day, much of their great wealth has never been found.

At first, Pizarro took brutal revenge for the continued resistance of the native population. He had thousands of the Incas killed. Then he tried a different strategy by giving full support to Manco, a younger brother of Atahualpa's foe, Huáscar. Taking Manco to the Inca capital city, Cuzco, Pizarro personally crowned him as "Lord Inca."

Pizarro also tried to stop his men from looting the Inca treasures, but they would not listen to him and continued stealing jewels from the temples, even opening graves to take gold and silver ornaments from the dead. After that, many of the conquistador warriors themselves managed to gain or lose fortunes in jewels,

This print from 1595 presents a completely idealized view of Cuzco. Although the city was laid out in a similar gridlike pattern, the main plaza was in the center and not on the side.

playing at dice with their comrades. Both of the Spanish leaders soon departed from Cuzco. Francisco Pizarro founded what would become a great city, known today as Lima, on Peru's Pacific coast. Meanwhile Almagro, dissatisfied with his share of the spoils, took his men to Chile, hoping to win still another vast fortune there.

Seeing his chance, Manco organized a powerful Inca army. By that time the natives had come to understand that the Spanish invaders were not in fact gods but, instead, were merely men who could, with spears and arrows, be made to bleed and to die.

First, from positions outside the city of Cuzco, Inca archers and slingers directed thousands of flaming objects into the thatched roofs and the sides of buildings. Before long, virtually the entire city was engulfed in fire. Many of the Spaniards burned to death. Others were caught in ropes thrown by the invaders and then carried away into the night. Manco, along with some of his closest followers, now copied his foes, leading the Inca attacks on horseback.

Outnumbered, and facing almost certain death, the conquistadores at Cuzco rallied, using cannon fire and ferocious charges by their cavalry. Finally, the Inca warriors fell back, pursued by the furious Spaniards. Their retreat soon became a rout, with the natives fleeing in total panic. Thousands of the Incas were slaughtered, their bodies then cut to pieces.

In the days that followed, fighting began again, this time taking the life of Francisco Pizarro's gentle and popular younger brother, Juan. Shortly afterward, at Lima, Pizarro himself launched a successful attack on the Incas who had surrounded his forces there. At last, in August 1536, Manco's warriors slowly withdrew from the scenes of battle, desperate to plant crops for the following year in order to survive.

By spring of the next year, the city of Cuzco fell to invaders, this time not to Incas but to the conquering force of Almagro, Pizarro's own partner and companion.

On horseback, Manco led the Incas'
attack against the Spaniards.

After the failure of his campaign in Chile, Almagro
determined to seize by force what he thought was his
fair share of Pizarro's conquests. Striking without warn-
ing, he captured Cuzco, taking as his prisoner
Hernando Pizarro, brother of the captain-general and
Almagro's longtime personal enemy.

To gain his brother's freedom Pizarro agreed that
Almagro could continue to control the city of Cuzco.
Then, Charles V would finally decide on the specific

52

areas of South America to be ruled by the two competing leaders.

Almagro faithfully lived up to the agreement, immediately freeing his enemy, Hernando. By contrast, soon after the two Pizarros were reunited, Francisco warned Almagro either to surrender the city of Cuzco at once or be prepared for deadly combat.

On April 26, 1538, the two armies met on an open field. From a nearby mountainside, crowds of Incas laughed loudly and cheered while watching the bloody combat. Spanish swords, lances, and bullets clanged against Spanish shields and armor. Hernando Pizarro's

*Almagro battles
Hernando Pizarro,
and takes him prisoner.*

force finally was victorious. In all, more than 150 conquistadores lost their lives in the struggle.

Almagro, old and sick, was imprisoned by his enemy. Then, following a mock trial, he was strangled to death. In a crowded public square, the smiling Hernando Pizarro watched with pleasure as the aged head of his brother's once-faithful comrade was severed by an ax and thrown into the mud.

Francisco Pizarro publicly praised his brother's deed. Then, acting without permission from the emperor, Pizarro claimed for himself all the territory that had belonged to his former comrade, Almagro. For that move he soon paid dearly. When his brother, Hernando, journeyed to Spain, Charles V ordered that in return for his selfish cruelty Hernando was to be imprisoned in a royal fortress for twenty years.

Meanwhile, the Inca leader, Manco, seeing the conquistadores in bitter conflict with each other, arranged lightninglike raids against plantations operated by the Spanish invaders.

Pizarro angrily imprisoned Manco's wife. Having her stripped naked, he ordered his men slowly to shoot her body full of arrows until she died. After that horrid act the Incas determined never to forgive the Spanish invaders and never to surrender to them.

Nor had the loyal followers of Almagro, Pizarro's former partner, forgiven the captain-general for permitting, and even praising, the murder of their leader. Since that killing, the Almagrists, unlike Pizarro's

*Pizarro is murdered by a band
of men loyal to Almagro.*

troops, had been reduced to poverty, even laughed at in the streets by soldiers in Pizarro's army. Finally, one group of angry Almagrists determined to gain revenge by murdering Francisco Pizarro himself. On June 26, 1541, they stormed through the gates of Pizarro's palace in Lima.

At the time, the Spanish captain-general was at lunch with some twenty friends. Hearing the attacking force approach, some of the soldiers dining with their commander, instead of defending him, escaped through windows. As Pizarro struggled to put on his armor, his brother, Martín, fought bravely against the band of assassins. They ruthlessly killed him, advancing quickly toward the commander.

Alone now, the elderly Pizarro fought with youthful skill, plunging his sword into two of the attackers. He then ran the sword into a third man. But before he could withdraw it, the mob descended upon him. As many as a dozen swords and knives cut into his body.

Falling to the floor, Pizarro called out the name of Jesus. With blood from his own wounds he drew a Christian cross on the floor and reached out to kiss it. But before he could do so, a final blow put an end to his extraordinary career.

CONCLUSION
PIZARRO
IN
HISTORY

Born to poverty, Francisco Pizarro never learned to sign his own name, never married, and cared little for elegant clothing or fancy food and drink. Eager to accumulate riches, he was uninterested in hoarding his wealth. Instead, he enjoyed the pleasure of spending it.

Like most of the Spanish conquistadores, Pizarro was a man of great courage. Yet, unlike so many of the others, after undertaking a task he felt obliged to complete it. He was constant in his purposes, unyielding, daring. Beginning with only a handful of troops, he managed somehow to conquer an empire.

But there was another side to the great conquistador. Pizarro sometimes lied to his partner, Almagro, and badly cheated him. He lied to Atahualpa and had him killed. He allowed his forces to rob the villages they conquered, to rape the women, and to turn the Inca people into slaves. In large part because of him, the paradise of Peru was turned into a land of hopelessness.

Driven both by ambition and by hunger for gold,

Pizarro succeeded. Wealth, power, and fame were his rewards. But, both for himself and for Peru, the price was terrible. At least for a time, the only winners were the rulers of Spain.

IMPORTANT DATES

*c.*1475	Probable date of Pizarro's birth, in Trujillo, Spain.
1513	Balboa discovers the Pacific; Pizarro at his side.
1519	Cortés welcomed to Tenochtitlán by Aztec ruler, Montezuma.
1521	Cortés finally conquers Tenochtitlán.
1524	Pizarro's first voyage along the Pacific coast of South America.
1526	Contract between Pizarro, Almagro, and Luque to divide profits of their enterprise in Peru.
1526–27	Pizarro's second voyage along the coast; draws line in the sand when ordered to return to Panama.
1529	Queen of Spain signs an agreement allowing Pizarro to conquer Peru.
1532–November 16	Capture of Atahualpa, ruler of the Incas.
1533–August 29	Atahualpa executed.
1533–December	Pizarro arranges for coronation of Manco.
1535–January 6	Lima, Peru, founded by Pizarro.
1538–July	Hernando Pizarro executes Almagro.
1541–July 26	Francisco Pizarro murdered by followers of Almagro's son.

FOR FURTHER READING

FOR OLDER READERS

Bingham, Hiram. *Lost City of the Incas*. New York: Duell, Sloan and Pearce, 1948.

Brundage, Burr Cartwright. *Empire of the Incas*. Norman, Okla.: University of Oklahoma Press, 1963.

Hemming, John. *The Conquest of the Incas*. New York: Harcourt, Brace, Jovanovich, 1970.

Lockhart, James. *The Men of Cajamarca: A Social and Biographical Study of the First Conquistadores of Peru*. Austin, Tex.: University of Texas Press, 1976.

Means, Philip Ainsworth. *Fall of the Inca Empire and Spanish Rule in Peru*. New York: Charles Scribner's Sons, 1932.

Prescott, William H. *History of the Conquest of Mexico and History of the Conquest of Peru*. New York: Random House, 1989.

FOR MIDDLE READERS

Bernhard, Brendan. *Pizarro, Orellana and the Exploration of the Amazon*. New York: Chelsea House, 1991.

Marrin, Albert. *Inca and Spaniard: Pizarro and the Conquest of Peru*. New York: Atheneum, 1989.

INDEX

Page numbers in *italics* refer to illustrations.

ABOUT
THE
AUTHOR

William Jay Jacobs has studied history at Harvard, Yale, and Princeton and holds a doctorate from Columbia. He has held fellowships with the Ford Foundation and the National Endowment for the Humanities and served as a Fulbright Fellow in India. In addition to broad teaching experience in public and private secondary schools, he has taught at Rutgers University, at Hunter College, and at Harvard. Dr. Jacobs presently is Visiting Fellow in the Department of History at Yale.

Among his previous books for young readers are biographies of such diverse personalities as Abraham Lincoln, Eleanor Roosevelt, Edgar Allan Poe, Hannibal, Hitler, and Mother Teresa. His *America's Story* and *History of the United States* are among the nation's most widely used textbooks.

In the Franklin Watts First Book series, he is the author of *Magellan, Cortés, Pizarro, La Salle, Champlain,* and *Coronado.*